OF THE SUN-KING

AN ADVENTURE
IN WHICH YOU ARE THE HERO

Dedication

To the two Jamies,
Brother and son.
One for Inspiration,
The other for fun.

Learning Development Aids
Duke Street
Wisbech
Cambs PE13 2AE
England

The Crown of the Sun-King Ref no. LD 782

ISBN 0-905114-2-48

THE CROWN OF THE SUN-KING

by
Dr Michael Thomson

with illustrations
by Tim Oliver

LDA

Learning Development Aids

Note for teachers, parents (and readers)

The Crown of the Sun-King is an exciting adventure story in which the reader is the central character. Adventure stories (such as those in the 'Fighting Fantasy' or 'Way of the Tiger' series) have proven highly popular with all age groups, but are too difficult for many pupils to read.

The Crown of the Sun-King is the second in a series of 3 adventure stories for poor and reluctant readers. It brings all the excitement of adventure stories within the grasp of the poorer reader. It has a controlled reading age (of about 9 years), with simple short sentences. The content and excitement is, however, for the older child, typically 12 and upwards through the teens.

Reading the Crown of the Sun-King

The reader begins at number one (opposite). Thereafter he or she makes decisions which determine which page is read next.

Readers will need:

A copy of the Adventure sheet at the back of this book. (This may be freely photocopied.) During their adventure readers will need to fight off many of the creatures they encounter. The Adventure sheet helps them to keep a record of their victories and losses.

2 Dice. Each time a reader fights a creature they will throw their two dice. The number they throw is entered in the 'Fighting Skills' column alongside the name of the creature. Pupils then add the dice throw to the number already in the column, which gives them a value for their fighting skills.

The story will tell them the fighting skill of the creature. The greater number wins.

A Pencil.

Each time a reader stops reading the Crown of the Sun-King, he or she must note the story number they have got to on their Adventure sheet. This will enable them to continue their adventure later.

Teachers may also find that pupils will enjoy writing about what has happened to them so far. This helps continuity and checks that readers are understanding what they are reading.

THE CROWN OF THE SUN-KING

1

You are in a castle. You have just come from a fight with Grom. Grom was the evil one that took the Secret Land from the Sun-King. You beat Grom. (Read about what happened in The Castle of Grom.)

Now you are able to be the star of another exciting adventure. Only you can find the Crown of the Sun-King.

You will need a copy of the Adventure Sheet at the back of this book.

(You can write in the book if it is your book. If not ask someone to photocopy it for you.) You also need a pencil and two dice.

You will visit many exciting places and you will meet many strange creatures. Some of the creatures are evil and will try to kill you. You will need to fight them. When you fight you will throw your dice and work out your fighting skill. The story will tell you when to fight.

Look at your Adventure sheet. It lists all the creatures you may have to fight. You may not meet all these creatures and you may not meet them in this order. Each time you fight a creature remember to fill in your Adventure sheet. The story will tell you how.

Sometimes you can choose to fight with Magic, Weapons or Combat. Choose wisely. Think about the creature you are fighting. Try to choose something he is not good at. The story will help.

Your adventure sheet also shows you that you have 25 Life Points. You may lose Life Points in your adventure. You may also be given some more. Be careful, if you lose all your Life Points you die!

Your Adventure sheet shows you that you have an equipment list. You will be given many useful things on your journey. Remember to write them on your Equipment List.

If you have read The Castle of Grom you will have useful equipment that you may need here. Copy your equipment list from The Castle of Grom Adventure sheet onto Crown of the Sun-King Adventure sheet.

Finally, remember to write down the number you are on when you finish reading. Do this in the 'story number' column on your Adventure sheet.

The people of the Castle are happy that Grom has been beaten. A man comes into the room. He bows. He says "Welcome, chosen one! Let me take you to the Hall. There you can choose to be the Ruler of the Secret Land. You will have to prove yourself a good and wise person".

The man is called Elgor. He used to help the Sun-King. Now he will help you. Elgor claps his hands. Six guards march in. They will take you to the Great Hall.

The guards form up beside you. You all march out. You go down a long passage. You enter a huge room. There are weapons around the wall. There are mats on the floor. The floor is made of wood. The guards move away from you and you see a tall man. He looks fit and strong. He has a thin sword. He is Gamesmaster. In a soft voice he asks you to fight him. You can ask the guards to take him—63, or you can fight him—112.

2

You walk into the flowers and dancing people. The flowers and people change. The land is rocky and grey. You have walked into a training ground for the Fell Lord's Army. All around are Orcs, Trolls, Goblins and other nasty creatures. It is a trap! Magic hid the

real look of what is here. You must take 2 Life points from your Life point score.

One creature looks at you. It is man-like with claws. It has eyes like bees' eyes, but much bigger—150.

3

The glow gets brighter. The Mace is now very bright. The light of the Mace helps you see well. You see something in a crack in the rock wall. It shines. You go over and see an axe in the crack. With a little work at the rock you pull it free. It is a very fine axe. It has a sharp blade. The blade is still shiny even after being hidden. The handle of the axe has many jewels set into it. It is a Battle-Axe. You take the Battle-Axe. Write it on your equipment list. You turn into the next passage—85.

4

You put down your weapons. You tell the dwarf that you will give him a fair fight for the Battle-Axe. The Dwarf is small but strong. He is also very tricky.

The **Dwarf King** has 12 Fighting skill points.

If you win—120. If you lose—71.

5

You take out the Mace of the Sun-King. Mace and Crown give off a flash of blue light. The Fell Lord takes a step back. Then the Crown goes red again. The Fell Lord takes out his sword. The Mace stays blue. You now can use Magic and Weapons at the same time. You draw the Sword of Prost. It glows blue. It stays blue! Prepare to fight the **Fell Lord.** Throw your dice and work out your fighting skill—73.

6

You go to an old river bed. It is cut into the side of the mountain. The river bed has sand and blue stones in it. You walk along the old river bed. You see that some of the stones shine. You bend down to look at one. It is a diamond! You see lots of diamonds. They are uncut but are still diamonds. You walk round a turn in the bed. There you see a mass of diamonds. Lying on top of this mass is a huge snake. It rises up over you. The snake's hood opens. It fixes you with its eyes. The eyes glow in an odd way. You find that you cannot speak. The snake's head sways from side to side. You find that you are going to sleep. You blink and shake your head to keep awake. You can speak no spell. The huge snake slides towards you. It is the **Serpent Guard.**

You must prepare to fight before you fall asleep. Throw your dice and work out your Fighting Skill.

Will you use Combat—28 or Weapons—61?

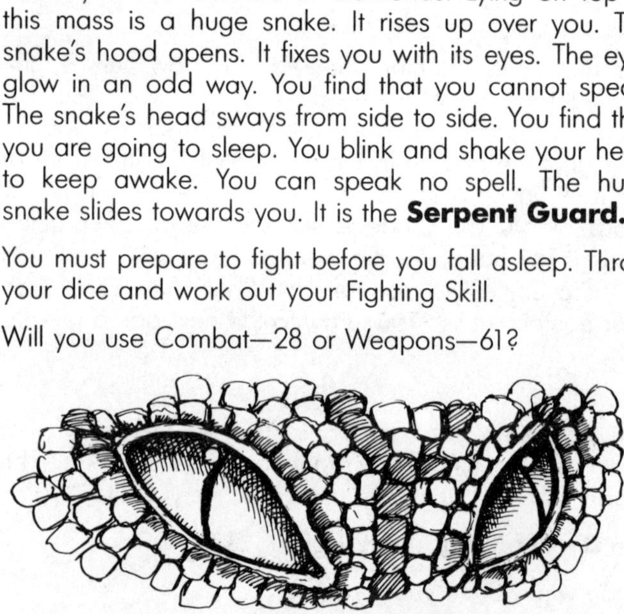

7

In the dim light of the passage you see a huge bulk. It seems like a man, but it is beast-like. He has a huge belly with arms and legs like tree trunks. He has a sharp twisted bit of iron in his hand. His face is lit up by evil and malice. It is the **Evil Jailor,** the creature that Grom gave his victims to after he had finished with them!

You must prepare to fight him. Throw your dice and work out your Fighting skill score.

He moves to attack you. You may choose Combat—38 or Weapons—77. You can use Magic only if you used the key to get out of the cell. If you used Magic to get out of the cell your magic powers need a rest. To fight with Magic—148.

8

You enter the dark passage. There is a feel of magic in the air. The air smells of rot. The walls of the passage feel wet. Then you find that you are in a huge room. Torches light up the room. They have flames that do not burn up the wood. You see a gold box. It is the size of a man. You are in the Tomb of the Sun-King! You see that the lid of the box is open. You look in and see a skeleton. You look for the Crown. You do not see the Crown. You do see a long rod with a jewel set at one end. It is the Mace of the Sun-King.

You reach out to take the Mace. Just as you are about to touch it a bony hand grabs your throat. Once again you cannot use a spell. You are about to choke! The skeleton will try to save the Mace. You can use Combat—44, Weapons—175 or pick up the Mace—104.

9

You take out your dagger. You are tired. The power of the red Crown is too great. Elgor stabs you with his own dagger. Red fire burns you up. You have failed at last! Your adventure ends here!

10

The Sword of Prost is broken. You use your dagger. The dagger passes into the shape. It does no harm. The shape has no body. Lose one Life point. You can try Combat—94 or Magic—162.

11

You climb over a pile of rocks. This takes you round the pit of lava. You jump down off the rocks. The rocks hid a band of Trolls who were going by. The Trolls are huge hairy brutes. They are short but very strong. They saw you on the rocks and lay in wait. When you jump down they grab you. Before you can do anything they put a gag in your mouth. You are also tied up. The Trolls then camp for the night. Over their meal they talk about you! Will they eat you or take you to the Fell Lord?

The Trolls post two guards. The rest go to sleep. They snore very loudly. You bite at your gag. After a time you work it loose. If you have a **call for help from the Dragons** (check your equipment list) —36. If you did not help the Dragons—146.

12

You walk on. You tell yourself that it is nothing to do with you. You hear the cries fade away. You then think that a true Ruler would care for all the people—98.

13

The glow gets dim. You come to another fork. Will you go left—57, or right—105?

14

You turn around quickly. There you see another dwarf. This dwarf has a thick black beard. He is younger than the old dwarf but looks strong. He has a gleam of fun in his eye. He looks at the lake and says, "You have seen my Lake." He then sees the Battle-axe you found. He says "You have also seen my axe". He tells you that he is the King of the Dwarves. He is leading the band who fight the Fell Lord. He then asks you for the Battle-Axe. Is the dwarf telling the truth or is he another greedy thief who wants the jewels on the axe? Are all dwarves like the old dwarf or are others honest and true? If you want to give the dwarf the Battle-Axe—122. If you refuse to give the dwarf the Battle-Axe—155.

15

You chant the Runes "INTRA HIC". The door opens and you see a dark passage in the mountain. You go in and make your way under the mountain. There are some cobwebs, but nothing else. You have made good time as you did not go back with Bork. The Fell Lord has not had time to post a guard here. You see a light at the end of the passage. You come out of the mountain—143.

16

You tell the dwarf that you will be glad to go with him. You walk on and the dwarf tells you many stories of dwarf history. The dwarf does not tell you of how often the dwarves are greedy. They lust after gold and jewels. When you make camp that night the old dwarf puts something to make you sleep well, into the drink. While you sleep he takes the diamonds. Cross them off your equipment list. You are left alone in the dark mines!—110.

17

You need to get past the Orcs and Trolls. You also need to get the guards away from the Red Way. Thon tells you that his party of dwarves is ready. They have been wanting to fight back. He tells you to stay. Thon goes off. Some time later you hear a blood chilling scream! It is Thon and his pack of dwarves. They rush into the cave. Thon whirls the Battle-Axe above his head. The Axe screams like something alive. Many of the Orcs and Trolls run. Those that stay are cut down by the dwarves. Thon kills many with the Battle-Axe. The guards join in the fight. You see your chance and run for the red way—62.

18

The ghost is your old friend the Sun-King. He is upset that you cast a spell on him. It is lucky that you only cast a spell to ward him off. As he stands still you see who it is. You undo the spell and say sorry. You are very glad to see him. Once again he will help you.

The Sun-King tells you the story of his power. He tells you that once, long ago, the first King of the Secret Land was walking by the sea. He saw an odd-looking woman. She was small, but gave out a feeling of great power. The woman's eyes were sea-green. When she looked at the King her eyes glowed. The King felt a mind of great power. The Sea-Woman told him to visit a certain sea cave. The cave was only open at low tide. When the King went in he found a Crown and a Mace. These were of shining gold, like the sun. The Crown gave the power of wise and strong rule to the King.

Since then all the rulers of the Secret Land, Kings or Queens, have had the Crown as the power for their rule.

The Sun-King had been the last ruler. Grom with his evil power had found out the secret of the Crown. He had made his attack when the Crown was not worn. The Crown was now lost. It is said that any who can prove to be wise and just may rule if they can find the Crown of the Sun-King. The Sun-King tells you he sees in you a good and wise ruler. All you need is the Crown. He then fades away.

You may add one Life point to your score.

You may start at once to look for the Crown—26, but you should go and look at the old dungeons if you have not done so—50.

19

One of the Dragons takes you back to the land near the Southern mountains. You feel a sense of something strange in the air. You see bands of Orcs going by. Sometimes there are creatures that have no name. They look evil and strong.

At last you come to the foot of the mountains. Here you see a bit of rock like a door. If you have the Runes from the twisted tree—78. If you do not have the Runes—45.

20

You move around each other. You feel a strike on your rib. You fight for breath. The Gamesmaster is very skilled. Just as he moves in for the final blow you twist to one side. This is a trick you saw Grom use! The Gamesmaster falls off balance. You drive in hard. He falls to the ground with a crash. As he falls he pulls you down! You lie there for a while panting—172.

21

You draw your sword and wait. The lead buffalo comes near you. You thrust the sword point into its eye. The point goes into the brain. The buffalo dies at once. He falls at your feet. Quickly you lie down so that the huge bulk of his body is between you and the herd. You hide behind the body of the lead buffalo. Like two streams of water the rest of the herd pass each side. None of them wish to trip over the body. The noise as they go by is loud. You are safe. After a long time all the herd go by and you go back to Bork. He is still asleep—179!

22

You go back to the village. You are angry with them for giving the girl (and others) to the Crab-Beast. You feel a vast power flow into you. You lift your hand and bring a fire down on the village. All are killed. As you leave the smoking village you think that the people were afraid. As they were weak they did the only thing they could. Perhaps you might have had pity—98.

23

You hand over the gold coin. Without a word the figure waves you onto the boat. You get in and the figure gets in too. It pushes off with a long pole. You talk to it in a friendly voice. It says nothing. You ask it if it would like to share some of your lunch. It does not speak. You sit back and enjoy the river. After a while the river begins to flow faster and faster. You hear the sound of fast running water—rapids ahead. You turn to tell the figure of the rapids. It has gone. The boat is tossed about like a cork. You are taken miles down the river and the boat crashes on some rocks. You are tossed ashore. You find that you are in the Dragon Wastes.

This is the burnt land where the Dragons live. As you lie in the sun to dry off you hear the sound of Dragon wings. You see a yellow Dragon land near you. It is Bork. He looks at you and says "So! We meet again you weak human. This time I do not have orders from the Dragon King." Bork flames a little at you. You say a spell that you found in a book of the Sun-King's. The spell stops Bork making any flames. Bork's mouth is shut up! Bork is very angry and comes at you.

You must fight **Bork**. Throw your dice and work out your Fighting skill. You can fight him with Combat—60, Weapons—37, or Magic—134. Think about what would surprise Bork.

24

You see the Orcs and Trolls by using the power of the Crown. They are afraid. The lovely face laughs. Then turns into an ugly shape. You have failed your first test. The Crown goes a deep red. The band crushes your head. You die! Your adventure ends here.

25

The Fell Captain is a magic creature. He has all the power of the Fell-Lord. There is only a small chance that you will win.

The **Fell Captain** has 23 Fighting skill points.

If you lose—33. If you win—80.

26

You go back to the Great Hall. There you meet with people from the lands all around the Castle. They are grateful for your work with Grom, but fear that you may be just as bad! You tell them that you will seek the Crown of the Sun-King to prove yourself.

You tell Elgor to act for you while you are away. He agrees at once. You walk awhile with the Gamesmaster before you go. He tells you of dark stories from the south. He also tells you of a place across the desert where the Sun-King's body is said to rest. You think that the Crown may be there. At least that is a good place to start. The Gamesmaster warns you against Elgor. You laugh at this saying that you must trust someone.

You take your leave and can go out into the forest path—93, or walk round by the moat to find a path there—152.

27

Elgor leads you to the Throne room. This is a great hall with the Throne of the Secret Land there. The room has some people in it. They look at you as you sit on the Throne. Then they look at Elgor. You tell them all about your adventures.

You also tell them about the Crown and the tests. You show them the Crown glowing blue.

Elgor says that he will be the first to call you the true Ruler. He then says that as you are tired you should rest. He will take the Crown to put in the Royal Safe. Will you give the Crown to Elgor and rest—95 or will you rest later and talk to the people now—55?

28

You take up your stance. It is a shame that the Serpent Guard is so strong. It also has the speed of all snakes. It makes a strike at you. Its forked tongue flicks out.

The **Serpent Guard** has 15 Fighting skill points.

If you win—171, if you lose—141.

29

You seem so weak and the Dragon is huge. Bork tears at you with his claws in a fit of rage. You are badly hurt, lose 2 Life Points—149.

30

The Evil Shape flows all around you. It tries to fill your mind. You feel dark going into you. The evil power is too great. The Crown turns red. It crushes your head. You have failed! Your adventure ends.

31

The cat does not seem to know much Magic. You chant a spell to make the two heads fight each other. You say "Heads right, now fight". The heads turn to each other.

The **Two Headed Guard Cat** has 12 Fighting skill points.

If you win—139. If you lose—72.

32

You take out the key and try it in the door. It fits! You open the door and go out—7.

33

The Fell Captain shouts with glee. The red sparks of his evil magic jolt you. You feel your life flow dying. You become one of the Fell Lord's creatures. This is the end of your adventure!

Next time use the **Mace.**

34

You rush into the cave. You stand in front of the girl. The crab-thing is very angry. Its huge claws open and close. It has a hard shell as its skin. Its sickly green eyes look down at you. Prepare to fight the **Crab-Beast.** Throw your dice and work out your Fighting skill. You can use Combat—108, Magic—39, Weapons—126.

35

The Fell Lord is weak. The power of the Crown fades from him. One blow sends him to the ground. As you bend over him hands grab you by the throat. With his last gasp he chokes you. You both lie dead on the ground! Your adventure ends!

36

You call out the word that the Dragon King gave you. The Dragons can hear this magical word. The Trolls cannot hear anything. It is not long before the Dragons come. They set upon the Trolls. The Trolls run off with their backsides on fire. The Dragons help you get the ropes off you. You thank the Dragons and they go off on their way. If you have a **map** (check your equipment list)—56. If you do not have a map—132.

37

You draw your sword. Dragons have hard skin. It is like scaly armour. They are also used to fighting with swords. This is because knights look for Dragons to fight all the time. This was a bad choice.

Bork has 15 Fighting skill points.

If you win—149. If you lose—29.

38

Not a good choice! The beast is huge and strong. Your best punches and kicks bounce off his belly. He laughs.

The **Evil Jailer** has 17 Fighting skill points.

If you win—130. If you lose—90.

39

A good choice. You try a Magic spell. The Crown lights up. the spell does not work. It seems that your test does not allow you to use Magic. Use Weapons—126, or Combat—108.

40

You leap to one side of the Serpent. Its head darts past you. A kick behind the head makes the Serpent stop dead. You hit again and its neck is broken. You take some of the **diamonds**. (Write them on your equipment list.) You go back to—179.

41

The glow gets brighter. You come to another fork. Will you go left—57 or right—105?

42

You go into a room on the left. It has a large window. The sun shines in. You see thick dust in the air that you have made by your feet on the floor. The dust makes you sneeze. The room has nothing in it. You go into the other room—127.

43

You follow the glow of the Mace to another cave. Here you see many Trolls and Orcs. At the end of the cave you see a way that is lit with a red light. You see some guards there. If Thon, the Dwarf-King is with you—17. If you killed the Dwarf King with the Battle-Axe—125.

44

You pull back from the coffin. The skeleton keeps his grip on your throat. You slash with the side of your hand. Bits of the skeleton fall to the ground. The hand still chokes you! Lose 2 Life points. You can reach for the Mace—104 or try Weapons—175.

45

You make the long trek back to Table-Top Mountain. You climb up the mountain. You visit the twisted tree and see Runes carved into it. They say "Intra Hic". Write **"Intra Hic"** on your equipment list and go back to the Southern Mountains—78.

46

You take your sword. With one blow you strike at Bork's throat. He makes a sad screaming noise. Before you kill him the Dragon King comes to see what the noise is. He is angry with you. His fiery breath scorches you. —Lose 4 Life points. You must spare Bork's life—113.

47

You go into the Castle. It seems very quiet. There is no one there to welcome you. You shout out. A face looks round a door. Then it moves away at once. After a time you hear the rush of feet coming downstairs. Elgor comes out of the doorway. It looks as if it has been a great surprise to see you. He frowns, then quickly smiles. He bows and tells you what a joy it is that you have come back. Elgor is dressed in very rich clothes. You can go to the throne room—27 or your bedroom—64.

48

This is not a good choice. Your best punch makes him grunt, but he comes on. The huge fist of the Troll crashes into your head. You fall to the ground. Lose 3 life points! You then try a Magic spell—164.

49

You try and cast a spell. You are tired. The red Crown's power is too great. Elgor lifts his hands. A red fire comes from them. It burns you up. You have failed at the last! Your adventure ends here!

50

You go to the old dungeons. You go down dark and steep stairs. You take a burning torch for lights. The dungeons are full of poor creatures from Grom's evil rule. Many are now dead from lack of food. Some have died in great pain. Those that are still alive you will set free. You look into one of the cells. There is a crash and clunk of a large key in the lock. The door slams shut. You are locked in the dungeon. You hear the sound of a laugh. It sounds vile and cruel. You rush at the door. It is firm. You see the skeleton of the last person who was in this cell! If you have a **key** on your Equipment List (from the Castle of Grom adventure) go to—32. If you do not have a key to go to—74.

51

The Fell Lord does not look so strong now. He looks smaller. He seems afraid. You lash out a hand.

The **Weak Fell Lord** has only 13 Fighting skills points this time. If you win—174. If you lose—35.

52

You take out the Silver Chains that Thon gave you. You throw them at Elgor. The chains seem to have a life of their own. The chains curl round Elgor. There is a flash of red light. The Crown now has no colour. Elgor has no power. You take the Crown from him. It lights up with a blue light. You take out the Mace. It also glows blue. You place Elgor's hands on it. You ask again where Gamesmaster is. Elgor tells you that he locked Gamesmaster up.

Elgor gives you the key to the dungeon that he has locked Gamesmaster in. He begs for mercy. You banish Elgor. You warn him that if he returns to the Secret Land he shall be killed—180.

53

You pick up the Crown. You also pick up the bits of the Sword of Prost. You put them in your pack. Write down the **Crown** and the **sword bits** on your Equipment List. You then think that you will have to try the crown on sooner or later. Why not now?—91.

54

You see a strange mound on the mountain top. You walk to it and see a hole in the side of the mound. The mound is very large. The hole has two large stones each side of it. It leads into the mound. The way in is dark. There is no sound. All the animals and birds are quiet. The mound seems very strange indeed! If you want to go into the dark passage—8. If you do not want to go in—179.

55

You start to talk to some people. You begin to tell them more of your quest. You become very sleepy. Your head drops. Then you doze off. You are so tired that you sleep.

You wake with a start! Elgor is in front of you. He has the Crown on his head. It has turned red. You feel evil power come from him. He wants to take the Crown from you. He has taken the Crown while you sleep. You ask him where Gamesmaster is. Elgor smiles and says that he has gone away. He then lifts his hands. If you have the **silver chains**—52. If not you can use Combat—133, Magic—49, Weapons—9.

56

You look at the map. It shows many paths. Most of them end in a rock wall. There are paths of lava too. You see a path on the map that goes out of a rock wall. You take this path—153.

57

The glow gets brighter. You come to another fork. Will you go left—3 or right—76.

58

Bork flames at one vulture. The other slashes at you with its sharp beak. It catches you on the side of the head. You lose your grip on Bork. You fall to your death.

59

By the side of the river you see a small lake. A waterfall goes into the lake. You hear a cry that seems to come from the waterfall. Someone calls for help. You can walk on—12, or go and see what the cry is—163.

60

You read, in the same book, that Dragons have poor eyesight. They also have weak necks. You will try to leap at Bork from behind and go for the neck. A good choice!

Bork has 11 Fighting skill points.

If you win—149. If you lose—29.

61

The Serpent Guard is very strong and quick. Your sword will even the odds.

The **Serpent Guard** has 11 Fighting skill points.

If you win—171. If you lose—141.

62

You go into a passage lit with a red glow. There is a sense of doom here. You feel that the light is pushing you back. You sense something fearful ahead. You come to the end of the passage. There, in a huge room, is the Fell Lord. He is seated at a table. He faces away from you. All you can see is his cloak and the back of his head. There is a crown on top of his head. It has blue and red lights in it. The lights are sometimes more red or sometimes more blue. The Fell Lord is reading a book of evil magic. He does not seem to know that you are there.

You creep up slowly behind him. You reach out to take the Crown. Then he turns! "Fool!" he sneers, "I have been waiting for you. My power is strong and I see far". The Fell Lord stands. He is a huge man with dark hair. His face looks as if it has seen much pain. There is also a sense of fear behind the evil in his eyes. He wears a cloak of black. There is a sword by his side.

"You will not have my Crown" he screams, "Die, now!" The Fell Lord spreads his hands wide. He points fingers at you. The Crown lights up all red. The light runs down his arm and into his hands. Then a red light like fire cracks at you from his fingers. The light hits you in the chest. You fall to the floor. Lose 2 Life points. If you are still alive to go—69.

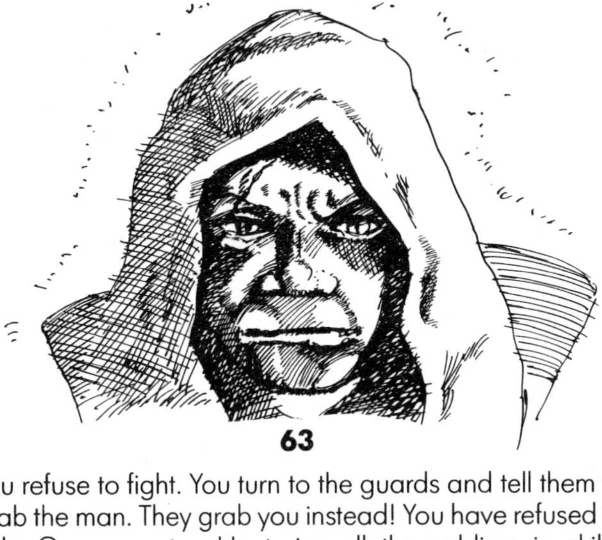

63

You refuse to fight. You turn to the guards and tell them to grab the man. They grab you instead! You have refused to fight Gamesmaster. He trains all the soldiers in skills. Gamesmaster says "You are not worthy to be ruler. You fail my test". The guards throw you into the castle moat. You drown!

64

Elgor leads you to your bedroom. It looks as if someone has been sleeping here while you were away. You tell Elgor about your adventures. You also tell him about the Crown. Elgor says that you must rest. He will take the Crown to put in the Royal Safe. Will you give the Crown to Elgor and rest—95, or will you rest later and see some more people now—55?

65

You thank the dwarf, but tell him that you will go on your own. The dwarf walks away. You think of all you have heard about dwarves. They can often be greedy. They lust after gold and jewels. That night you camp in the mines. The old dwarf has been following you. While you sleep he steals the **diamonds**. Cross them off your Equipment List. You are in the dark mines alone!—110.

66

One of the Crab-Beast's claws reaches out for you. You roll to one side. Too slow! The claws close on your body. You are cut in two. You do not live for long. The Crab-Beast has two meals now! Your adventure ends!

67

You notice that the Mace glows. You walk down the passage. The glow gets dim. You walk the other way and the glow gets brighter. Will the Mace take you to where you want to go or will it led you into a trap? If you want to follow the Mace—123. If you do not want to follow the Mace—173.

68

The **Vulture** has 11 Fighting skill points.

If you win—178. If you lose—58.

69

The Fell Lord mocks you. "So, you would take the Crown!" he says. He then tells you that he was one of the Sun-King's knights. When Grom came and killed the Sun-King he took the Crown for himself. Since then his power has been growing. He then takes up his hands once more. Just as you seem about to die the Crown changes. For a short space of time it goes all blue. You must act now! Will you hold up the Mace of the Sun-King—5 draw the Sword of Prost—136 or try a Magic spell—111?

70

You have no way of opening the door. You will have to take the time to go all the way back to Table-Top Mountain and visit the twisted tree—45.

71

The Dwarf flips into the air. He turns over and gives you a blow on the head as he goes by. He is now behind you and gives you a punch to the kidneys. You turn and the Dwarf King gets close in. He gives you a bear hug. This drives all the breath from your body. You give in. The Dwarf stands back. You rest. The Dwarf asks you again for the Battle-Axe. You can give the Axe to him—122 or fight him with Weapons—106.

72

The cat is far too quick for you. You hear a rasp of hot air on your back. The cat has jumped over you. It is now behind you. You feel claws rake your back. Lose 4 Life points—140.

73

The sword of the Fell Lord has two edges. The Crown now glows with a red fire. The fire flows down the Fell Lord's arm to the sword. The Sword of Prost glows with a blue fire. The Fell Lord lifts his sword with a shout. He strikes. You block with the Sword of Prost. A crash sounds. Sparks of blue and red flame fall all around. You feel a shock up your arm as the two swords clash once more.

The **Fell Lord** has 27 fighting skill points.

If you win—138. If you lose—157.

74

You see that you will have to break the door down. You chant a spell of breaking. "Door shake, wood break". You hear the door groan. You take a deep breath and leap. Your flying kick smashes the door down. The spell and your kick have taken a lot out of you. Lose 2 Life points. You go out of the smashed door—7.

75

You untie the girl. She tells you that she was tied up by her village. Every year they give someone to the Crab-Beast. The person is chosen by lot. If someone was not given to the Crab-Beast it would eat all the people in the village. The people were fearful and have no weapons. They did not want to do it but had no fighters. You hear the story out. You can go and destroy the village for giving the girl to the Crab-Beast—22, or you can tell them they need fear no more—158.

76

The Mace gets dim. You think you see a large creature hurry down another passage. Will you go left—41, or right—13?

77

You draw your sword. The Sword of Prost glows blue as it feels the evil of this beast. You strike and the twisted iron meets the sword. Sparks fly! The bit of iron has some power too! The Evil Jailer does not seem too good at using it.

The **Evil Jailer** has only 11 Fighting skill points.

If you win—130. If you lose—90.

78

You chant the Runes **"Intra Hic".** The door opens. You see a dark passage going under the mountain. You walk in. After you have walked a little way you hear a growl. There is some light from the door. You have taken too long to get here. The Fell Lord has had time to post a guard. You see a huge cat-like animal. It has two heads. Both the heads are looking at you! The cat-like animal looks very quick and strong. It is the **Two Headed Guard Cat**. You will have to fight. Throw your dice and work out your fighting skill score. Will you use Combat—119, Weapons—84 or Magic—31.

79

You call for Bork. He is still taking his nap. Dragons sleep well. He does hear you at last! He flies quickly to you. He comes just in time to see you crushed to death by the buffalo herd!

80

The Fell Captain shouts. The red sparks of the evil magic fly around you. The air smells of burning. Your blows give off a blue light. The red and blue mix. The blue wins out. Your blows now send the Fell Captain back. He screams and then is no longer there. The training ground is also gone. You can see the creatures no more. Add 2 Life points to your score.

You now see that the mountains have many caves and passages in them. You go into one of the caves—103.

81

You take a big log that you see there. You slide the log over the pit of lava. You walk across with care. The lava is very hot. If you fall in, you will be burnt to death. At last you reach the other side. You then find the path. On the path is the Troll. He is part of a band of Trolls. He runs at you waving a huge fist. You have no time to draw your sword. But you must fight The **Lone Troll**. Throw your dice and work out your Fighting skill. The Troll looks very strong. Will you use Combat—48, or Magic—164?

82

You see a cloud of dust far away. You leave Bork to take a nap. You walk a little way to the dust. It seems to get closer. You can hear a sound like many drums. Then, you can see them! Many cow-like creatures on the move. It is a herd of buffalo! The buffalo were stranded on Table-Top Mountain before the mountain rose above the desert. Now they are in a stampede. You are in the way of this stampede. You will be crushed under their flying hooves. You can call out a magic spell to stop them—109, stand your ground and cut down the lead buffalo with your sword—21, or call for Bork to fly you out of there—79.

83

You find that all the Orcs and Trolls have gone back to their own land. You see a lot of Dwarves. There is Thon the Dwarf King. He is very pleased that the Fell Lord is dead. He gives you a present of some silver chains. He says that they can stop even very strong magic. He also tells you that you can call on him to set the mines right. Write down the **silver chains** on your Equipment List. You then leave the mines to make your way back to he Castle—144.

84

You take out your sword. The cat is strong and quick. There is a chance that you might beat it.

The **Two-Headed Guard Cat** has 15 Fighting skill points.

If you win—139. If you lose—72.

85

The passage leads into a cave. The cave is large with a high roof. You see a lake here in the cave. The water of the lake looks cold and dark. The light from the Mace shines on the lake. You are very thirsty. Will you take a drink from the lake—118? If you do not want to take a drink from the lake go to 177.

86

You walk along the bank of the river for a while. You come to a place where a boat rests. You are just about to get in when a figure appears. It is in a robe with a hood. You cannot see a face under the hood. It is all dark. The figure reaches out. The hand that reaches out from the robe is the hand of a skeleton. The bones of the hand open. The figure wants money for the boat. Check your Equipment List. If you have a **gold coin** you may go to—23. If you do not have a gold coin go to—151.

87

You run back to the village. While you go back for help the Crab-thing eats the girl. You then think that a true ruler would act quickly when needed. Anyway, the people tell you that they will not help. They have to give up someone from the village every year. If they do not, the Crab will eat them all. You should have seen that there was something odd about the girl being tied up!—98.

88

You take out the diamonds. They shine with a strange light. All around the flowers and people change. You see what they really are. The diamonds have helped you see past the magic. The land is really like the grey and rocky land that you have come past. The people are Orcs, Trolls, Goblins and other nasty things. It is a training ground for the Fell Lord's Army. You hide behind a rock. A man-like thing with claws looks around. It lifts its huge nose. It sniffs. It's eyes are like bees' eyes, but much bigger. It looks at the rock you hide behind. The creature can sense you. With a huge bound it runs to you—150.

89

You strike home. The Knight runs off. You look to see what the others are doing—131.

90

The Evil Jailer comes on at you. He grunts like a pig. He is so keen to get you into his dungeons that he loses all fear. Your strikes do not slow him. A mighty blow sends you into the wall. You are in a daze. The Jailer thrusts you into another cell. This one is all metal. It has no key as it is bolted from the outside. It has letters carved into the door. This makes it spell proof. You are stuck in here for ever at the mercy of the Jailer!

91

You pick up the Crown. You put it on your head. At first you feel power flow into you. Add 5 Life points to your Life point score. At once the Mace and the broken bits of the Sword of Prost glow blue, then red, then blue. The Crown is like a hot band around your head. You feel ill. Your head hurts. You see a green-eyed woman. She has a kind face. It seems a dream. She says that the Crown will test you. If you pass the test you will be a fit Ruler. The Crown will then turn blue and you will have great power. If you fail, the

Crown will turn red and you will die. The Crown will crush your head.

You try to take the Crown off—it is stuck on!

Again, as if in a dream, the woman is gone. You see another face. This one is very lovely. The fair face says "What the woman says is not true. You can trust me. Am I not fair to look at?" The face then tells you to use the power of the Crown to make all the Orcs and Trolls your slaves. Will you do what the face says—24, or will you refuse—142?

92

You meet a Mad Knight. He charges at you on his horse. The Dragons are fighting other Knights. Prepare to fight the **Mad Knight**. Throw your dice and work out your Fighting skill score. You can use Combat 129, Weapons—168, or Magic—116.

93

You walk down the path to the forest. After a time you come to a river—86.

94

You strike out with a body blow. The shape has no body. Your hit passes through it. Lose 1 Life point. You can try Weapons—10 or Magic—162.

95

You give the Crown to Elgor. You ask him where Gamesmaster is. Elgor says that he has gone away. He smiles in a strange way. Then Elgor puts the Crown on his own head. At once the Crown glows red. Elgor seems to grow and you feel a great evil power there. Elgor plans to take the Crown from you. If you have the **Silver Chains**—52. If not, you must try Magic—49, Combat—133, or Weapons—9.

96

You accept the test. You throw down your sword. The man does the same. Just as you start to move to him he gives a great shout! It is the shout of 'akai'! You are struck still. Lose 2 Life points as his fist hits your head! You now strike back! Use your Fighting skill points.

Gamesmaster has 12 Fighting skill points. If you have 12 or more you win, if you have less than 12 you lose.

If you win—20. If you lose—156.

97

You go back up the stairs. If you have heard the story of the Sun-King's power you can go to—26. If you have not heard this story you must go on to other parts of the Castle—102.

98

You fail the test. The Crown is now a deep red. You feel a hot pain inside your head. You fall down. When you wake you have no recall of anything. You wander the lands, a nameless tramp, until you die. Your adventure ends. You have failed.

99

Your spell works. The Troll hits himself hard with his own fist. He falls to the ground. You walk on. Add one to your Life point score.

You see some paper that sticks out of the Troll's pack. You take it out. It is a map! Write the **map** down on your Equipment List.

You go on. The path comes to a dead end. There is now no way to go on. You go back to the lava pit and cross the log. You will have to climb over the rocks after all—11.

100

You chant a spell. The ghost lifts a hand and points at you.

The **Ghost** has 10 Fighting skill points.

If you win—18. If you lose—166.

101

The Knight is too quick for you. He runs his lance into your belly. A painful death!

102

You go to the old keep of the castle. This is a square tower. It is on a hill and is on its own. It has been empty for years. You climb the dusty stairs. When you reach the top of the stairs you see two doors. You can go in the left hand door—42 or in the right-hand door—127.

103

The cave leads into a long passage. The walls look as if they are man-made. You come to another passage that goes across. There you see a light coming down the passage. The light gets closer. You make out a child-like figure. When the figure reaches you it is a dwarf, not a child. It is a very old dwarf. He has a twisted smile on his lips. The dwarf's eyes shine in the light of the torch he is carrying.

The dwarf greets you. He tells you that you are in the old mines of the dwarves. Once, gold, silver and jewels were mined. Now the Fell Lord has made the dwarves into slaves. The mines are no longer worked. Evil creatures stalk the mines. The old dwarf tells you that he is part of a band who have got away. They now try to fight the Fell Lord. He asks you if you have any gold or jewels. He says these will help in the fight. You show him the diamonds. The old dwarf says that he will take you to the others. You can then find the Fell Lord. If you want to go with the Dwarf—16. If you do not want to go with him, go on your own—65.

104

You grab the Mace. The jewel lights up. The hand of the skeleton drops away. The skeleton falls into dust. The spell only makes the skeleton save what is in the coffin. Once the Mace has been taken the spell is broken. As you walk back you think about where the Crown is. You also think what powers the **Mace** might have. (Write it on your Equipment List.) Add one point to your Life point score. Go to 179.

105

The Mace gets dim. You come to another fork. Will you go left—57, or right—13.

106

The Dwarf stands looking at you. You pick up the Battle-Axe and bring it down onto his head. The Dwarf King has no Fighting skill points and he cannot stop you. He falls to the ground. The Dwarf King is dead. You feel that you have done an evil act. You hope that you will not have to pay for this later—43.

107

The Fell Captain is very handy with the Club. He has magic helping his weapon skills. There is only a small chance that you will win.

The **Fell Captain** has 22 Fighting skill points.

If you lose—33. If you win—80.

108

Was this wise? The crab-thing is very strong with a hard shell! You slash out with a flying kick. You hurt your foot.

The **Crab-Beast** has 20 Fighting skill points.

If you win—114. If you lose—66.

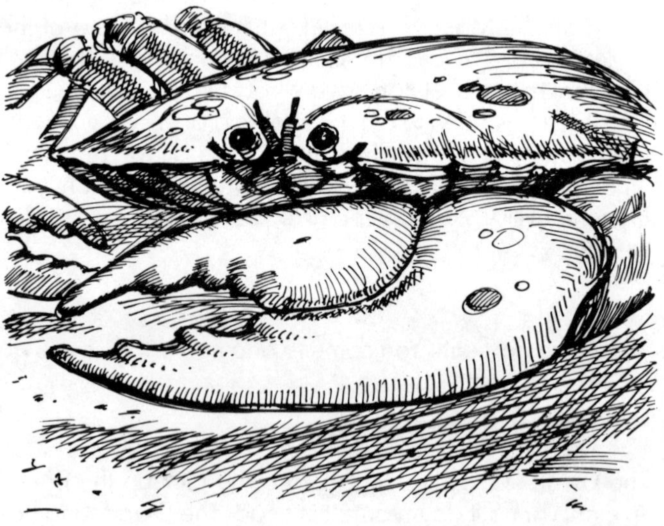

109

You chant a magic spell of stopping. "Legs numb, don't run". Some of the buffalo at the front of the herd crash to the ground. The buffalo behind cannot get out of the way. There are too many in front of them. They crash on to the fallen buffalo. More buffalo behind them keep going. They come to you. Your magic does not have the power to stop all of a buffalo herd. There are too many of them. You are crushed to death!

110

The next morning you awake. You find that the diamonds have gone. You curse all Dwarves. You now have to find a way onward. If you have the **Mace** of the Sun-King—67. If you do not have the mace—145.

111

You begin to chant a Magic spell. Then the Crown changes to red. The Fell Lord lifts his hands. A blast of red fire strikes you again. Lose 2 Life points. If you are still alive you can draw the Sword of Prost—136, or hold up the Mace of the Sun-King—5.

112

Prepare to fight **Gamesmaster**. Throw your dice and note the number. Now work out your Fighting skill. You are ready to fight—96.

113

You let go of Bork and grant him his life. Bork is sorry that he lost his temper. He tells you that he was only having a little fun with his flame. He was going to make you hot, not hurt you. You make friends. You tell Bork about your quest for the Crown of the Sun-King. Bork says that he will help you. He will be your flying steed! You get up onto Bork's back. Bork leaps into the air. You are away up into the sky. You enjoy flying along. Bork seems to enjoy having you along too.

You fly over the desert. There is nothing to be seen but sand and bare rock for miles. The sun overhead is very hot. You are glad of the wind. You see two black specks in the sky ahead. The specks get closer. The specks turn out to be two huge birds. The birds have sharp beaks and heads with skin, not feathers. They are after your flesh. Bork goes for one. Prepare to fight the other **Vulture**. Throw your dice and work out your Fighting skill—68.

114

One of the Crab-Beast's claws reaches out for you. You roll to one side. The claw closes. If you had been inside it you would have been sliced in two. You see that the eyes are the only weak spot. You roll again. Then you get to your feet. You leap up and land on the Crab-Beast's back. You strike hard onto the left eye. Then the right eye. The force of your blows reaches the Crab-Beast's brain. It dies. You leap clear as it falls. You then go over to the girl—75.

115

The Troll swings the axe so fast that he falls to one side. You see his left side open for a sword thrust. The Troll falls to the ground and you take your sword out of his side. The other Trolls are still asleep. You can add two to your Life point score. You creep away from the Trolls' camp.

If you have a **map** (check your Equipment List)—56. If you do not have a map—132.

116

You chant a spell "Mad knight, cannot fight". You hope he will run off!

The **Mad Knight** has 10 Fighting skill points.

If you win—89. If you lose 101.

117

You go on alone. Bork says goodbye and flies off. You walk across a land of woods and fields. There is a feel of fear in the air. Now and then you see bands of Orcs in the distance. You also see other things. They have no name, but look evil and strange—137.

118

You take a drink from the dark lake. The water is so cold that you gasp. Then you feel the drink chill you. Just as you think that you have made a mistake the water warms inside you. You feel a strong jolt of power. The water is from the Lake of the Dwarf King. It is well known for its powers. You may add 5 Life points to your Life Point score. The water has given you a strong life force.

Then you hear a noise behind you—14.

119

Oh dear! The cat is very quick. As you get ready it has jumped at you. It twists in mid-air to land behind you.

The **Two-Headed Guard Cat** has 18 Fighting skill points.

If you win—139. If you lose—72.

120

The Dwarf flips up into the air. He turns over and gives you a blow on the head as he goes by. He is now behind you and gives you a punch to the kidneys. You turn and the Dwarf King tries to get close. He will give you a bear hug. This is a well-known Dwarf act. It will drive the breath from you. Before he gets close you fling yourself on to one side. A kick sends him flying. You follow up with a lock on his neck. The dwarf gives in. You let him stand. The Dwarf asks you again for the Battle-Axe! You can now give it to him—122 or fight him with Weapons—106.

121

The next day you say goodbye to the Elves. Once again you fly off with Bork. You have not gone far when you see another Dragon. The Dragon soon comes near you. It tells of an attack on the Dragon Home. Mad Knights have attacked the Dragons. Bork has had many fights with Knights and the Dragon asks him to help. Bork says that he must go back to help out. You may go on alone—117, or go back with Bork and help him fight the Mad Knights—161.

122

You give the dwarf the battle-axe. The dwarf thanks you. He is really the King of the Dwarves. He tells you that his name is Thon, son of Binth, son of Roth, son of....... You quickly tell him of the old Dwarf before he goes on for ever with the history of the Dwarf Kings. Thon is shocked when he hears your tale. He tells you that he is sorry. He says that on behalf of all the dwarves he will make up for the old dwarf. You tell him of your search for the Crown. He tells you that the Fell Lord's power comes from a crown he wears. He says that he will help you in the fight. He tells you that the Dwarf King's Battle-Axe that you gave back has some power.

"Now", says Thon. "It is time to rest before the battle!" He soon has a fire going. He takes out some food from his pack. You share the Dwarf King's meal. Thon eats as much as five men. There is still some left for you. Thon also takes out some wine. This makes him very friendly. He tells long tales of Dwarf history. You fall asleep. Thon does not seem to notice. He carries on telling his tales.

In the morning you wake up feeling rested. You may add 4 Life points to your Life points score. You set off with Thon. You follow the Mace to the Fell Lord—43.

123

You follow the Mace. It seems that if you go nearer to the Crown the Mace will get brighter. If it goes away from the Crown it will get less bright. The Crown must be near for the Mace to light up in the first place. You come to a fork in the passage. Will you go left—41, or right—13?

124

You see a strange tree ahead of you. It is twisted and has no leaves. As you get near the tree you see letters carved on the bark. The tree has Runes or magic letters carved on it. The Runes say **"Intra Hic".** Write down these Runes on your Equipment List. You then go back to where Bork waits—179.

125

You need to get past the Orcs and Trolls. The guards also need moving from the red way. You have no help. You feel the mind of the Fell Lord seeking. He seeks out the evil of your killing the Dwarf King. He sees you. Many of the Trolls and Orcs are sent for you. They attack. You fight off many but you feel swords and claws bite into you. At last you get free. You run and hide. You are tired and bleeding. Lose 8 Life points. If you are still alive you creep past the guards into the red way—62.

126

The Sword of Prost is broken in bits! You will have to use your dagger. You will have to find a way past the claws and hard shell.

The **Crab-Beast** has 16 Fighting skill points.

If you win—114. If you lose—66.

127

You go into a room on the right. There are no windows here. It is very dark and cold. The dust makes you sneeze. Just as you turn to go you hear a sound. It seems as if you heard someone say "Hello!" You see a glow in the corner of the room. It is as if the dust shines in the dark. It takes the form of a ghost-like shape. The mouth opens and closes in an odd way. You feel the hairs on the back of your neck rise up. You cannot fight a ghost with Combat or Weapons. You chant a spell. The ghost lifts a hand up and points at you.

Prepare to fight the **Ghost**. Throw your dice and work out your Fighting skill—100.

128

You will find that all the Orcs and Trolls have gone back to their own land. You see a lot of dwarves. They are pleased that the Fell Lord is dead. They can have their mines back. They are not so pleased with the death of their King. They bind you in magic silver chains. The Crown now has no power. You die an old man after many years as the captive of the Dwarves.

129

You flip over in the air. You try to land on the Knight's back.

The **Mad Knight** has only 10 Fighting skill points.

If you win—89. If you lose—101.

130

The Evil Jailer comes at you. He grunts like a pig. He looks as if he would like you in his dungeons for good. He is so keen to get at you that he loses all fear. Lucky for you this makes him lose all his skills too! He is slow. Your quick strikes come at him too fast. He seems upset! Then it is too late. He lies still on the ground. As he falls a **Gold coin** rolls out of his pocket. It has a strange boat on it. Take it and write it on your Equipment List. Go to—97.

131

You are sad to hear that Bork has been killed. The Mad Knights have been beaten. The Dragon King is grateful for your help. He says that you may have one **call for help from the dragons** if you ever need it. Make a note of this on your Equipment List—19.

132

You do not know where to go next. You walk all over the dry and dusty land. You try to find a path that does not lead to a dead end. All you find are rock walls and lava. You get very tired. Lose 2 Life points. At last, by luck, you find a way. You go into a pass set in a rock wall—153.

133

You are tired. The red Crown's power is too great. Elgor hits you with the back of his hand. Red Fire burns you up. You have failed at the last! Your adventure ends here!

134

You start to cast a spell. Your Magic skills need a rest. You have just used a spell on Bork. Also, Dragons have magic of their own. This was a very bad choice!—29.

135

The **First Troll** has 11 Fighting skill points. If you lose—159.

If you win you must prepare to fight the **Second Troll**. He is approaching fast. Throw your dice and work out your Fighting skill—147.

136

You start to take out the Sword of Prost. It glows blue. Then the Crown changes to red. The Sword feels burning hot. You let go of it. The Sword drops back into its sheath. Once again the Fell Lord lifts his hands. You can try a magic spell—111 or hold up the Mace of the Sun-King—5.

137

At last you come to the Southern Mountains. They are very high. You see a part of the rock face that seems like a door. Just as you go near a large bird flies down. It is a talking raven. It tells you that the Dragons are safe. It also tells you that Bork has been killed. This makes you very sad.

You go on to the door in the mountain. If you have the Runes from the twisted tree (Intra-Hic) go to—15. If you do not have the Runes go to—70.

138

Each time the swords meet there are more sparks. Each time you feel a shock. The Magic of the Swords fills the air with a hum. The swords flash to and fro. At last you see that the Fell Lord's sword lights up bright red one last time. It meets the Sword of Prost. There is a great BANG! Red and blue lights up the room. The Fell Lord's sword is no longer there. The Sword of Prost is broken! The blade is broken in bits. The Fell Lord falls back. The Crown is now dim. You see blue flashes in it.

The Fell Lord is now weak. Prepare to fight the **Weak Fell Lord.** Throw your dice and work out your Fighting skill score—51.

139

The Guard Cat turns round and round. It growls and howls. It seems to think that one of its heads is another cat. While it is chasing itself you strike. The cat falls to the ground. Add one to your Life point score.

You walk on under the mountain. It gets very dark. There are some cobwebs but no more creatures. At last you see a light at the end of the passage. You go out into the Southern Land—143.

140

You move to one side and stop in surprise. The cat is attacking itself!—139.

141

The strike of the Serpent is too quick for you. You feel its fangs on your arm. The poison works very quickly.

Lose 4 Life points—154.

142

You say that no one shall be a slave of another. The face snarls and turns into an ugly shape. The shape gets bigger and bigger. It seems real. Prepare to fight the **Evil Shape.** Throw your dice and work out your Fighting skill score.

You can use Combat—94, Magic—162, or Weapons—10.

143

You walk out into the Southern Lands. Here the land is harsh. There are very few plants. The land has rocks and ash all over it. What was once a lush and green place is now dry and grey. Volcanoes belch out smoke, ash and lava. This is the work of the Fell Lord. Many of his creatures are going to invade the Secret Land. The Fell Lord wants to be ruler of all. Then all other lands will be like this. It looks like hell on earth!

You look ahead and see more mountains. You see a path. There is a pit of red hot lava between you and the path. You can go round the pit and climb over a pile of rocks—11. You can place a log over the pit to get to the path—81.

144

You come out of Dwarf Mountain. It is a long way back. This time there is no Dragon to fly on. You think about the Crown. It is now in your pack. Will you be able to pass the next test to prove yourself?

After some days of travel you see the Castle ahead. Behind you is Table-Top Mountain. You have seen nothing odd on your way back. The towns and villages you passed were friendly. You make yourself known to the people. They are all happy now that Grom and the Fell Lord are no more. You come to a river—59.

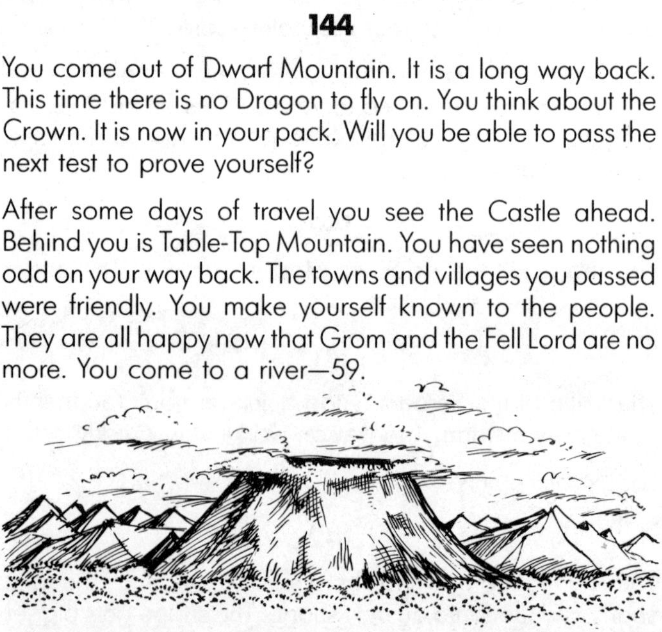

145

You lose your way in the dark mines. You find your way back. You will have to get the Mace. You go back to the Table-Top Mountain. After a long climb you start again from this point. You look around the mountain—179.

146

After an even longer time you work the rope loose. All the Trolls are still sleeping apart from the two guards. You get up and creep up to them. Just as you get near them they see you. You chant "Don't hoot, Trolls mute!" This magic spell stops the Trolls calling out. This means that you have used your Magic skills at this time. One of the guards has your sword. This is the one you go for first. Prepare to fight the **First Troll.** Throw your dice and work out your Fighting skill—135.

147

Before the Troll has time to do anything you strike. You punch into his belly. The Troll's breath comes out with a whoosh! The Troll leans forward just as your foot rises up. He is left in the dust. You take your sword from the Trolls pack and turn. The other Troll is slow to move (all Trolls are a bit slow). You wave the sword at him. He takes out a huge axe. The Troll swings it round and round. You try and get a sword thrust in.

The **Second Troll** has 11 Fighting skill points.

If you win—115. If you lose—159.

148

You chant a spell. The Evil Jailer seems a little fearful. Magic was the way Grom made it do what he wanted it to. He comes at you. You chant "Beast still, by my will". You take out your magic Sword of Prost, just in case!

The **Evil Jailer** has only 11 Fighting skill points.

If you win—130. If you lose—90.

149

Bork is in such a rage that he is careless. You leap up at him. You then turn over in mid-air. You are now behind him. Bork does not see you. Then you are at his throat. This is the Dragon's weak spot. You can add one point to your Life point score. You can kill Bork—46, or you can spare him—113.

150

The creature stares at you with those odd eyes. A feeling of great evil comes from him. You feel a cold fear fill your mind. The creature is in charge of all the others. He is the Fell Captain. He is a creature of magic, yet also very strong. He grins at you with sharp teeth. He takes out a vast club. It has nails on the end of it. He lifts it up with great skill. If you have the Mace of the Sun-King—170. If not, you must fight the **Fell Captain**. Throw your dice and work out your Fighting skill.

You can choose Combat—176, Weapons—107, or Magic—25.

151

You tell the figure that you have no money. The figure shakes its head. You do not want to start a fight over such a small thing. You go back to the castle to get some money. You get lost and find yourself outside the old dungeons—50.

152

You walk round by the moat. You see part of the moat flow into a river—86.

153

You come out of the pass in the rock wall. You see a green and lovely field. There are flowers growing. Little people dance and sing. Everything looks good. You think that it is strange that the dust and lava have gone. Where are the

Fell Lord's creatures? Can what you see be real? If you have any **diamonds** (check your Equipment List)—88. If you do not have any diamonds—2.

154

In a last desperate effort you leap at the serpent—40.

155

You refuse to give the dwarf the Battle-Axe. The Dwarf is very upset. He says it is his. He will fight you for it. The Dwarf has no weapons. You do not want to use any Magic here. The Fell Lord will notice. Prepare to fight the **Dwarf King**. Throw your dice and work out your Fighting skill. You can put down your own weapons and fight by Combat—4, or you can use Weapons—106.

156

The blow on the head has made you dizzy. The Gamesmaster strikes to a rib. He is very skilled. You fight to get your breath. You twist to one side. This is a trick that you saw Grom use! The Gamesmaster smiles and twists with you. A final crash and you are on the floor. As you fall you pull him down too. You lie there a while panting—172.

157

Each time the swords meet there are more sparks. Each time you feel a shock. You become tired. The Fell Lord does not seem to tire. He laughs as the Crown glows a brighter red. A final blow gets past your sword. You see the Mace and the Sword turn red as you die.

158

You take the girl back to the village. You tell them that they need fear the Crab-Beast no more. They are happy but weep for the years gone past. You see that the village people did the only thing that they could. They were weak and afraid. They had no one to turn to. You tell them that you will give each village help when you are Ruler. You leave the village after a feast. You feel a little tired as there was much drinking and dancing!—167.

159

The Troll gives you a blow on the head. He grins as you shake your head. A second blow crashes into you. The last thing you see is the Troll looking down at you. Will he eat you for tea? Your adventure ends!

160

You think there is something familiar about this ghost—18.

161

You go back to the Dragon Home with Bork. You help fight the Mad Knights—92.

162

The shape has no body. Combat and Weapons cannot help. Use Magic!

The **Evil Shape** has 14 Fighting skill points.

If you win—169. If you lose—30.

163

You go to the waterfall. The waterfall comes out over the rocks. Behind the waterfall is a cave. It is hidden by the water. You climb up the rocks. There, in the cave, you see a huge crab-like thing. It has large claws and is about to eat a young girl. The girl is tied to a stake in the cave. She sees you. So does the crab-thing. The girl tells you to go and save yourself. The crab-thing will eat her anyway she says. You can go back out of the cave and walk away—12, or you can fight the Crab-thing—34.

164

The Troll is very close. You chant "Lose your health, punch yourself". You hope to make him hit himself.

The **Lone Troll** has 11 Fighting skill points.

If you win—99. If you lose—159.

165

You wake Bork up from the nap that he is taking. You get on his back again and fly off. After a while you are not over the desert. You see a wood below. It is getting late. You need to take a rest and stop for the night. You see wood smoke below. Before you can say anything Bork is flying down. He has smelt something good. You find that the campfire has been made by Elves. They are very fair and have golden eyes. Bork knows most of them. They sing and dance around the fire. You may add 4 to your Life point score. The food and rest have helped a lot!

Late in the night one of the elves tells a dark tale. He says that stories have come from the south of nasty creatures. It is said that an evil lord has found some great power. He calls himself the Fell Lord. Stories are of torn land and of Dwarves being slaves. The Elves say that unless the Fell Lord's power is soon ended he will come north to the other lands. It may even be too late to stop him.

You go to sleep that night full of these tales. You have bad dreams of evil faces and smoke—121.

166

Your spell starts to shake the glowing dust. The ghost is very angry at your attack!—160.

167

As you walk on you hear the Crown hum. It shines a bright blue. You have passed all the tests. You were wise. You showed that you cared for the people by taking note of the call for help. You showed that you could think quickly and act when needed. You showed that you were brave by fighting the Crab-Beast without Magic. You showed good fighting skills. At the last you showed that you could show pity and were wise to your people's problems. You will be a good, wise and brave Ruler it seems!

The Crown glows blue and shines on your head. You feel a sense of strength flow into you. Not for battle but a happy and strong sense of power. You walk up to the Castle. It is now your Castle! You walk into the gates—47.

168

You draw your sword. The Knight comes at you with his lance. He is trained in Weapons.

The **Mad Knight** has 13 Fighting skill points.

If you win—89. If you lose—101.

169

The shape seems to flow all around you. It tries to fill your mind. You keep your mind clear. You chant your own name over and over. At last the shape thins out. It blows away like mist in the sun. You have passed your first test. The Crown glows blue. You feel a great power flow into you. You may add 6 Life points to your Life points score. Write down the **Crown** and the **broken bits of the Sword of Prost** on your Equipment List. You then go out of the cave—83.

170

You take out the Mace of the Sun-King. It shines with a bright light. It has Magic of its own. The Magic of the Mace helps you. You draw the Sword. It hums with power. The Fell Captain takes a step back.

Your sword crashes into the creature's club. Sparks fly off. You feel a jolt in your arm. The creature screams but comes at you again—80.

171

You draw your sword. The magic of the Sword of Prost helps you shake off the sleepy feeling. The Serpent strikes quickly. Its fangs drip poison. You leap to one side. You slice down across its neck with the sword. The head is cleanly cut off. The head of the Serpent flies over the ground. Add one point to your Life point score. You also take some of the **diamonds**. (Write them down on your Equipment List.) You walk back to the top of the mountain—179.

172

You both stand and grin at each other. The Gamesmaster says "You have proved that you are not afraid. You also have some skill!" The Gamesmaster trains the soldiers in all forms of fighting. He is a master of many kinds of Combat and Weapons. He will become your friend and helper. For now you can add 3 Life points to your score.

Elgor and the guards take you to your room to rest. You are given a meal and made to feel at home.

Elgor tells you that you could become the Ruler of the Secret Land. The Sun-King, before his death at the hands of Grom, said that anyone who freed his people could claim the throne. Elgor tells you that you need to be strong to keep the throne. There are many who would take it. As he speaks you see an odd look in his face. This is soon hidden by a smile and an offer of wine.

The next morning you think that it will be a good idea to look at the Castle. If it is to be yours you will need to know all you can about it. You can go to the old dungeons—50 or the old keep— 102.

173

You take no notice of the Mace. Sometimes it gets dim. Sometimes it gets bright. You walk down and up the passages. You get lost. Lose 2 Life points as you get tired. After a while you think that the Mace's glow must mean something— 123.

174

The Fell Lord is weak. The power of the Crown fades for him. One blow sends him to the ground. He now seems a normal man. He waves you to him. You bend down so that you can hear him. He says that he only wanted to do good at first. The Crown picks up the good and evil in your mind. He was too greedy and unkind. The Crown picked this up. It turns you to good or evil. It depends which is the strongest in your mind. The Crown turns red for evil power and blue for good power. He tells you to beware of the Crown's power. The man then dies. The Crown falls off him. There it lies. It has blue and red in it. If you want to put the Crown on your head—91.

If you do not want to put the Crown on—53.

175

You take out your Sword and hack at the skeleton. Bits of the skeleton fall to the floor. The hand still chokes you. Lose 2 Life points.

You can grab the Mace—104, or try Combat—44.

176

The creature is very strong and has magic helping his strength. There is only a small chance that you will win.

The **Fell Captain** has 22 Fighting skill points.

If you lose—33. If you win—80.

177

You do not take a drink. You are still thirsty. You hear a noise behind you—14.

178

Bork flames at one Vulture. It catches fire. The other slashes at you with its sharp beak. You duck. You hack at its wing with your sword. The Vulture gives a harsh cry and flaps away. It does not fly well. You fly on. After a while you see a large mountain. It sticks out of the desert like a cake on a table. All around is flat. The mountain has steep sides like cliffs. The top is flat. The flat mountain top must be many, many miles long. It is the Table-Top Mountain.

Bork lands on top of the mountain. You get off and look around—179.

179

You can go to the Dried Up River—6.

To the Twisted Tree—124.

To the Earth Mound—54.

Back to Bork and fly away—165.

To the Dust Cloud—82.

180

You go back down the dungeons. There you find Gamesmaster. He is very thin from lack of food. He tells you that Elgor has been plotting to be ruler. After you had gone for a while Elgor told everyone that you were dead. He also said that the Crown had been lost. Elgor made himself ruler. The people in the Throne were there to make him ruler. They are the Knights of the Secret Land. When Gamesmaster said that Elgor was not the rightful king, Elgor locked him up.

You go back to the Throne room. There the Knights wait. Gamesmaster points to the blue glow of the Crown. He says, "There sits the Crown of the Sun-King. This person has passed the tests. He is our rightful ruler." The Knights cheer. Then, one by one, they promise to be true to the Crown. You promise to do all you can to rule wisely. The Crown now fades to a narrow band around your head. It looks like a thick blue head-band. No-one would guess its power. The Crown, Mace and the Sword of Prost are all part of the same set of Magic items. You have done well. It is a pity that the Sword of Prost is broken! There may be people who can help you mend it. Then you would be unbeatable. But that is another adventure!

THE CROWN OF THE SUN-KING ADVENTURE SHEET

Name: Adam ....

Each time you fight you must work out your Fighting Skill Points.

You have already been given some Fighting Skill Points for each fight	+	Throw both your dice and write down the total number you have thrown.	=	Add these numbers together to find your Fighting Skill Points.
Skill Points given 6	+	Dice Throw 6	=	Your Fighting Skill Points

You win if you have the same or more Fighting Skill Points than the Creature.

You lose if you have less Fighting Skill Points than the Creature.

Creature	Skill Points		Dice Throw		Your Fighting Skill Points	Creatures Fighting Skill Points	Win/Lose
Gamesmaster	6	+	6	=	12	12	WIN

Life Points	Equipment List	Story Number
25	Spear	
	Magic flute	
	globe of riddles	

Bork	8 + =		
Vulture	6 + =		
Serpent Guard	7 + =		
Mad Knight	6 + =		
Two-Headed Guard Cat	9 + =		
Lone Troll	6 + =		
1st Troll	6 + =		
2nd Troll	8 + =		
Fell Captain	12 + =		
Dwarf King	4 + =		
Fell Lord	20 + =		
Weak Fell Lord	10 + =		
Evil Shape	9 + =		
Crab-Beast	11 + =		